BUILDING AMERICA

THE FORTS

BUILDING AMERICA

THE FORTS

Raymond Bial

BENCHMARK BOOKS

MARSHALL CAVENDISH

NEW YORK

Benchmark Books
Marshall Cavendish
99 White Plains Road
Tarrytown, New York 10591-9001
Website: www.marshallcavendish.com

Book design by Clair Moritz-Magnesio

Library of Congress Cataloging-in-Publication Data
Bial, Raymond.
    The forts / by Raymond Bial.
        p. cm. — (Building America)
    Includes bibliographical references and index.
    ISBN 0-7614-1334-0
      1. Fortification—United States—History—Juvenile literature. 2. Historic sites—United States—Juvenile literature. 3. United States—History, Local—Juvenile literature. 4. United States—History, Military—Juvenile literature. 5. Frontier and pioneer life—United States—Juvenile literature. [1. Fortification. 2. Historic sites. 3. United States—History.] I. Title.

E159 .B53 2001
973—dc21

                                                                                00-065079

Photo Research by Candlepants, Inc.
Cover Photo: Raymond Bial

The photographs in this book are used by permission and through the courtesy of:
The Granger Collection: 2, 13, 14, 18-19, 26-27, 28, 34, 36-37, 40. Raymond Bial: 6-7, 8, 10-11, 12, 16 (top & bottom), 17 (top & bottom), 44-45, 46 (top & bottom), 47 (top & bottom). Hulton Getty/Archive Photos: 22, 24-25, 32, 42-43, 48-49. Corbis/Bettmann: 30-31.

Printed in Hong Kong
6 5 4 3 2 1

Contents

Many native peoples of eastern North America, such as the Cherokee, built walls called palisades around their villages.

INTRODUCTION

"Europe stretches to the Alleghenies . . . America lies beyond."
— Ralph Waldo Emerson

For thousands of years, people have built forts and taken shelter within their walls. Bands of early people first gathered in caves to defend themselves against enemies and wild animals. They also camped on hilltops from which they could better protect themselves against attack. As people became skilled with stone and wood, they constructed walls around their camps, which came to be known as forts. The word *fort* comes from the Latin word *fortis*, meaning "strong."

Long before Europeans set foot in North America, many native peoples made their homes within forts. Eastern Woodland tribes—the Cherokee in the Southeast, the Huron in the Georgian Bay region of Canada, and the tribes of the Iroquois League—built palisades, walls

Early Pueblo people entered their fortress-like homes by climbing up ladders placed against the thick adobe walls.

of sharpened vertical logs around their longhouses. Often, they designed the entrance within a maze to confuse enemies who might invade the village. Along the inside walls, they erected platforms that served as lookout posts.

Ancient cliff-dwelling Pueblo peoples known as the Anasazi, or "Ancient Ones," also lived in fortlike homes perched on canyon cliffs in the desert Southwest. It was nearly impossible for enemies to scale these high walls. Made of stone or adobe, Pueblo homes had no windows, and a smoke hole in the roof served as the doorway. To enter, people climbed a ladder on the side of the house and descended another ladder through the smokehole. If attacked, they raised the ladders to prevent the enemy from getting into their homes.

When European explorers arrived in the Americas, they were awed by both the vast riches and the dangers of the continent. Spanish explorers ventured into Mexico, the Southwest, and Florida in hopes of finding gold. The French established posts along the St. Lawrence River and developed a lucrative trade in beaver pelts and other furs. The English colonized the seacoast from present-day Georgia to the Maritime Provinces of Canada, and the Dutch settled in New Amsterdam. The newcomers had firearms and cannons, weapons that offered an advantage when confronting Native American warriors. Yet the European powers had only a weak hold in the New World. They fought Indian tribes that resisted their arrival and battled each other for control of the continent. To protect explorers, traders, and colonists, they built forts such as Jamestown, the first permanent British settlement in North America, in strategic locations on harbors and at the mouths of rivers. The French established massive fortresses along the St. Lawrence, as did the Spanish in Florida and on the Gulf of Mexico.

Colonists at Jamestown built their houses within the walls of the fort located along the
James River in Virginia.

1

COLONIAL FORTS

Early North American forts had many forms. With scant money and little manpower, builders had to improvise by using logs or stone—whatever material happened to be at hand. Yet the challenges helped adventurous people come to terms with the unknown land. Erected in Virginia in 1607, the Jamestown fort was triangular in shape and made with logs and soil, both of which were readily available on the low river plain. To build a palisade, upright logs were driven into the ground. The wall on one side of the fort was about 140 yards long. The other two sides were each about 100 yards long. Each point had a bastion, a sort of tower, made of palisades and filled with packed soil. In the middle of the fort, a cannon pointed toward the gate, ready to blast any intruder. The walls also sheltered a church, small thatched houses, and a well. Within the walls, over one hundred English colonists made their homes.

In Florida, the Spanish favored stone. They built forts similar to

Cannons pointing over the walls were effective in defending the fort at Jamestown from attack by hostile natives.

In the struggle for control of North America, the Spanish built an important fort near St. Augustine to protect their claim to Florida.

the stone castles in their homeland and the stone forts the conquistadors had built in Central America and Mexico. On occasion, ships brought cargos of heavy stones all the way from Spain. However, Castillo de San Marcos Fort near St. Augustine, Florida, was made from coquina, a stone quarried from the bed of the ocean. With four diamond-shaped bastions and thick walls, this impressive fort was surrounded by a moat. Although pivotal in the British and Spanish struggle for North America, this fort was never captured. Far away, in the dry Southwest, the Spanish

When the British defeated the French at Quebec, all of New France—from the St. Lawrence to the Mississippi River—became British territory.

learned from the Pueblo Indians to make sun-dried adobe bricks. They stacked the bricks, applied mud mortar, and covered them with a layer of clay to make walls and rectangular buildings with rounded corners. Adobe construction was used to make houses, missions (Spanish churches), and forts.

The French established small posts along the St. Lawrence River. Built by explorer Jacques Cartier in the 1540s, one of the earliest forts became the city of Quebec in Canada. Situated high on a bluff, this fort was laid out in a semicircle, with palisades facing away from the cliff. The fort had a sturdy door and four embrasures, or flared openings in the walls, for cannons. Angling wide on the inside so soldiers could fire weapons easily, the embrasures narrowed to small openings on the outside to protect those within the fort. By the 1600s, this fort had grown to include an armory, living quarters, and workshops built of vertical planks. Placing planks or boards vertically became a distinctive French style. Along the inside walls of the fort was a parapet, or balcony. Soldiers could fire guns through loopholes in the wall. A gate and a drawbridge over a ditch offered further protection. A triangular bastion of earth was revetted, or strengthened and held together, by logs on which cannons were positioned. A dovecote supplied the troops with fresh meat, and a garden provided vegetables and herbs. In 1690, Sir William Phipps led the Boston militia in a failed attack on the fort at Quebec, the French capital of Canada. By then the fort had grown into a city—what is now the walled Upper Town—with impressive buildings and gateways.

Over time, the French strung trading posts westward along the shores of the Great Lakes. Explorers and traders known as voyageurs paddled birch bark canoes from one post to another, following the ancestral trading routes of the Huron and Ojibwe peoples. Much of this region was blanketed with a thick forest, and these frontier forts served as links along the international trade network in beaver pelts. And the forts themselves became the scene of lively commerce, as the French swapped glass beads and iron kettles for the Indians' furs.

In the 1750s, the French built Fort de Chartres near the Mississippi River, not far from St. Louis. Briefly renamed Fort Cavendish when the British took possession in 1765, the impressive stone structure features high walls, thick wooden doors, parapets, and embrasures for firing cannons.

The French also brought Jesuit missionaries, or Black Robes, who sought to convert the native peoples. They established churches in forts, such as Sainte Marie Among the Hurons near Georgian Bay. In December 1679, René-Robert Cavelier, Sieur de La Salle, and Henry de Tonty traveled by canoe with Father Hennepin and other priests into what became known as the Illinois country. La Salle hoped to establish a

string of French forts from an outpost on the southern edge of Lake Michigan, now the site of Chicago, along the Illinois and Mississippi Rivers, and all the way to the Gulf of Mexico. Reaching the mouth of the Mississippi River on April 9, 1682, he claimed the sprawling lands in the name of Louis XIV, king of France, and named them Louisiana.

New France included all the land drained by the Mississippi River

French and British traders paddled canoes to isolated posts deep in the North American wilderness.

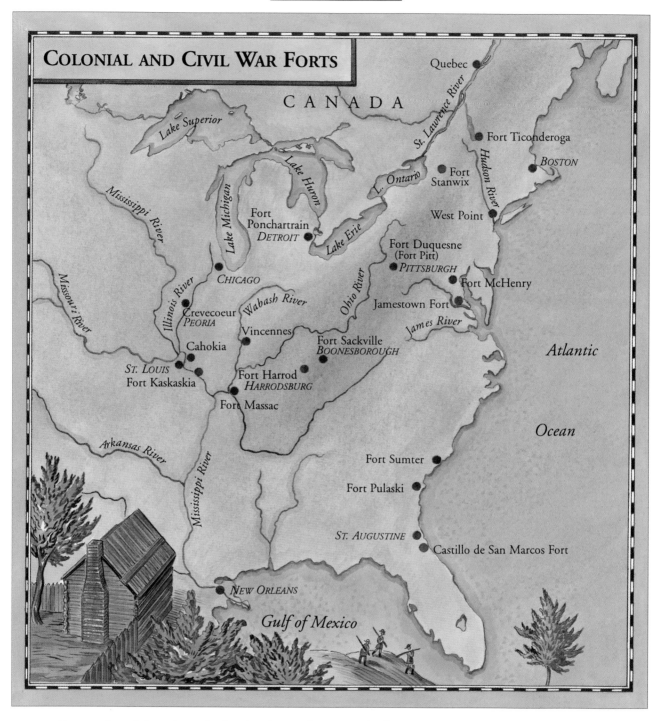

COLONIAL AND CIVIL WAR FORTS

CANADA

Quebec

Lake Superior

St. Lawrence River

Fort Ticonderoga

BOSTON

Lake Huron

L. Ontario

Fort Stanwix

Hudson River

Mississippi River

Lake Michigan

Lake Erie

West Point

Fort Ponchartrain
DETROIT

Fort Duquesne
(Fort Pitt)
PITTSBURGH

Fort McHenry

Missouri River

Illinois River

CHICAGO

Wabash River

Ohio River

Jamestown Fort

Crevecoeur
PEORIA

Vincennes

Fort Sackville
BOONESBOROUGH

James River

Atlantic

Cahokia

ST. LOUIS
Fort Kaskaskia

Fort Harrod
HARRODSBURG

Fort Massac

Ocean

Arkansas River

Mississippi River

Fort Sumter

Fort Pulaski

ST. AUGUSTINE

Castillo de San Marcos Fort

NEW ORLEANS

Gulf of Mexico

*From colonial days through the Civil War, forts were built as far west as the
Mississippi River at strategic locations on harbors and along rivers.*

from Canada to New Orleans. The great explorer La Salle attempted to bring this vast region under French control through a network of forts but was shot in the back by one of his own men before he could fully achieve his dream. Yet, Fort Crèvecoeur, meaning "broken heart," was built on the Illinois River near present-day Peoria and named in honor of La Salle's efforts. A stockade was later built nearby at Starved Rock. French forts were built at Kaskaskia and Cahokia, near the site of ancient Indian mounds along the Mississippi River near St. Louis. A fort was also built on the Wabash River at Vincennes, now part of Indiana. By the mid-1700s, log forts linked Fort Ponchartrain in Detroit with the infant city of New Orleans, as the French battled the British for the heartland of North America.

Through the Hudson's Bay Company, the British also sought their share of the fur trade. They established outposts in the northern reaches of Canada and at Hudson Bay and competed with the French. Notable among the outposts was Fort Nelson, a wooden stockade where the York River flows into Hudson Bay. Although this post could withstand Inuit attacks, it was manned by traders, not soldiers. In 1696, the fort fell to the French. For most of the 1700s, the French ruled the interior of North America, and their flag waved over many wilderness forts. Little villages had grown around each fort as French women and children settled in New France, realizing at least part of La Salle's plan. Native Americans camped near the forts, which had also become trading posts for furs and other goods. The French got along fairly well with the native peoples, and many trappers and traders married Indian women. In the meantime, the British were pushing westward into the Illinois country.

In 1755, competition between the French and the British for land and trade routes led to the French and Indian War. The French had fewer settlers than the British and could not defend their sprawling territory. Two of the most pivotal outposts in this conflict were Fort Stanwix, built by American colonists in New York, and Fort Duquesne, a British

In 1755, Native Americans ambushed and defeated British general Edward Braddock and his troops in Pennsylvania as they attempted to take Fort Duquesne.

outpost that was occupied and renamed by the French in 1754 at the present site of Pittsburgh. Both were strategically located on rivers, where they dominated travel and communication. They also served as bases for military campaigns in the wilderness. In 1755, Captain Dumas led nine hundred French and Indian troops from Fort Duquesne across the Monogahela River and attacked General Braddock's force of fourteen hundred soldiers. Just three years later, the British under General John Forbes took Fort Duquesne, which was rebuilt and renamed Fort Pitt after British statesman William Pitt. The bustling city of Pittsburgh later grew around the site of the fort. Both forts had bastions in each corner. Fort Stanwix had walls of horizontal logs strengthened with earthen banks. At ground level, there were gun ports and loopholes for muskets, with cannons over the bastion parapets. A square blockhouse fortified the bridge over a ditch.

La Salle's dream of French glory in the New World ended with the Treaty of Paris in 1763. French land east of the Mississippi was then surrendered to England while the land to the west was given to Spain. Pontiac, the great Ottawa chief, formed an alliance of Algonquian tribes to continue the war with the British colonists. However, the Native Americans' cause was ultimately lost when Pontiac was murdered by another Indian near Cahokia, Illinois, in 1769. The British finally took over the forts, though many French people continued to live near them.

A band of Native Americans gazes across the frozen river at Fort Clark, a frontier fort on the northern plains.

2

FRONTIER FORTS

The Atlantic seacoast was the frontier of the British colonies, and people would have remained huddled at the edge of the water, if forts had not been built in the interior. These included small forts, trading posts, and eventually the American cavalry forts of the Far West. As settlers gradually pushed westward over the Appalachian Mountains, forts were placed along rough trails through the wilderness. These forts protected the settlers' land claims on the frontier. Without them, few settlers would have dared venture into thick forests and parched deserts. A family could retreat to the fort if a band of Indians descended upon their homestead. The fort also served as a base from which soldiers battled Indians and as a stepping-stone for the pioneers crossing the new land. These frontier forts played a key role in the settle-

ment of America—a locus for both great historical moments and everyday lives long before the colonies won their independence from England.

Blockhouses were common in forts on the American frontier. Either square or rectangular and about twenty by thirty feet, their walls of

This drawing shows Fort Boonesborough in 1778, before an Indian attack.

Daniel Boone
blazed a trail through
the Cumberland Gap into
eastern Kentucky, where he
established the settlement of Fort
Boonesborough.

horizontal timbers were thick enough to stop musket balls. The ground floor had cannon ports and a row of loopholes. A ladder led through a trapdoor to the larger second level, which overhung the lower floor. Here were the officers' quarters, along with gun ports and loopholes for light weapons. Holes were bored in the wooden plank floor, so troops could fire down on anyone who broke into the room below. A steep roof kept snow from accumulating and repelled flaming arrows. Typically about thirty-five feet high, the blockhouse could shelter as many as a hundred men in an emergency, often the entire garrison stationed at the post. However, all the men were seldom at the fort at one time. Some were scouting the surrounding forests and prairies and sleeping out in the open.

Led by James Harrod, the first Kentucky settlers floated down the Ohio River in 1774. Upon reaching their destination, they immediately unpacked their axes and began chopping down trees. Soon they had log cabins for shelter and a palisaded fort to protect themselves from Indian attack. Fort Harrod became Harrodsburg, the oldest town in Kentucky. Daniel Boone and other frontiersmen were meanwhile blazing a trail known as the Wilderness Road through the Cumberland Gap, a pass through the Appalachian Mountains where the present states of Kentucky, Virginia, and Tennessee meet. Previously, settlers had come down the Ohio and Kentucky Rivers. Located on the Cumberland Trail, Fort Harrod guarded the best route through the Appalachians. In the summer of 1775, Daniel Boone established another important Kentucky settlement at Boonesborough.

Key battles of both the French and Indian War and the American Revolution were fought at Fort Ticonderoga in New York.

3

THE AMERICAN REVOLUTION

The outcome of the American Revolution was influenced by key Patriot assaults on eastern forts, particularly in New York at Ticonderoga and West Point and on Iroquois villages and British forts in the heartland. Throughout the war, the Iroquois had been killing settlers on the western edge of the colonies. To defeat the Iroquois, George Washington knew that their fortified villages had to be destroyed. So he ordered an all-out campaign in which soldiers did not pursue the elusive warriors. Instead they burned their palisaded villages to the ground.

George Rogers Clark, a lanky frontiersman with fiery red hair and beard, knew the war had to be won in the west—by seizing the British forts previously controlled by the French. He convinced the leaders of Virginia to permit him to form and equip a militia. Clark took his men down the Ohio River, secretly trained them, and journeyed to the British-held Fort Kaskaskia situated on a high bluff overlooking the Mississippi River in southern Illinois. Although he had only 178 men armed with long rifles, tomahawks, and knives, he knew that France had allied with the colonists in the revolution. Traveling overland from Fort Massac on the Ohio River, he slipped into Fort Kaskaskia at night and on July 4, 1778, took the stronghold, without firing a single shot. Upon learning that the rough and rugged militiamen were now their allies, the French residents of the fort became sympathetic to the American cause. Two days later, Clark took Cahokia, fifty miles up the wide, muddy Mississippi River, again without incident. He was helped by a French priest who went ahead and told the people they would not be harmed if they surrendered quietly.

The daring Clark now turned his attention to Fort Sackville in Vincennes along the Wabash River. Again a French priest went ahead and informed the inhabitants that the French were now allied with the American colonists against the British. Clark sent Captain Leonard Helm and twenty-five men, who easily took the fort. However, at the end of their short enlistments, some of the Americans went home, leaving Clark with a smaller force. In the meantime, Clark convinced a large group of Indians at Cahokia that the Americans were now friends of their French allies and therefore should not be attacked. Upon returning to Fort Kaskaskia, however, he learned that the British general, Henry Hamilton, had led a force of eighty soldiers to Fort Sackville and recaptured it. Helm was now his prisoner.

In a sweeping campaign during the American Revolution, George Rogers Clark captured the British-held outpost of Kaskaskia.

The Americans knew that Hamilton planned to drive them out of Cahokia and Kaskaskia in the spring. Clark would have to act quickly. On February 4, 1779, he fitted a keelboat with six small cannons and supplies. He sent the keelboat under the command of his cousin John

In their daring attack on Vincennes, George Rogers Clark and his men waded through the icy floodwaters of the Wabash River.

Rogers down the Mississippi, Ohio, and Wabash Rivers to meet his men just below Vincennes. Clark then led his band of ragged soldiers through a cold, driving rain over the prairies and through the woodlands of Illinois. With the early thaw, the men had to wade through flooded rivers. On February 13, they reached the Little Wabash and the Wabash Rivers, both of which were flooded, their waters spreading over their banks in a great sheet. They waited for the keelboat that was to carry them over the flooded lowlands, but it never came. Later, they would learn that Indians had attacked the keelboat and killed John Rogers. Unable to wait any longer, the men waded chest-high through the icy water, while holding their rifles and gunpowder over their heads.

Surrounding Fort Sackville, Clark and his men attacked, shooting their rifles with such accuracy at the loopholes that the British could scarcely fire back. The starving, tattered band of Americans was nearly out of ammunition, but General Hamilton was convinced they were a large force. With the British safely inside the log walls, Clark was at a serious disadvantage. However, he captured some of the Indian allies of the British. In full view of his opponents, he tomahawked one Indian after another, promising to smash open the heads of the British troops if they did not give up. Hamilton promptly surrendered on February 25, 1779.

In one sweeping campaign, George Rogers Clark had taken the western frontier for the Americans. With the capture of three strategic forts, Illinois country—the entire West at that time—was won for the United States. At the end of the American Revolution, settlers would no longer be confined to the eastern seaboard, but could move into the frontier in hopes of a better life. Yet once the American colonies had won their independence from Britain, forts were still needed to protect settlers pushing their way west.

During the War of 1812, the bombardment of Fort McHenry at Baltimore stirred Francis Scott Key to write the words to "The Star-Spangled Banner."

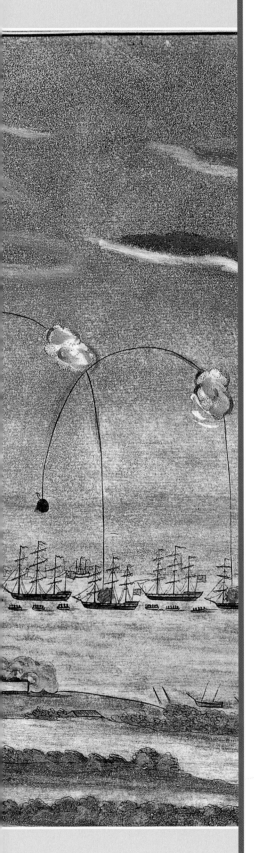

4

THE GROWTH OF THE NATION

Throughout the nineteenth century, forts continued to play a pivotal role in the growth of the United States. In the War of 1812, considered the second war of independence from Great Britain, Fort McHenry became especially famous. This war, the only time a foreign power has invaded the United States, began on June 18, 1812. Under the command of Major George Armistead, Fort McHenry needed a flag to fly over its walls in the Baltimore

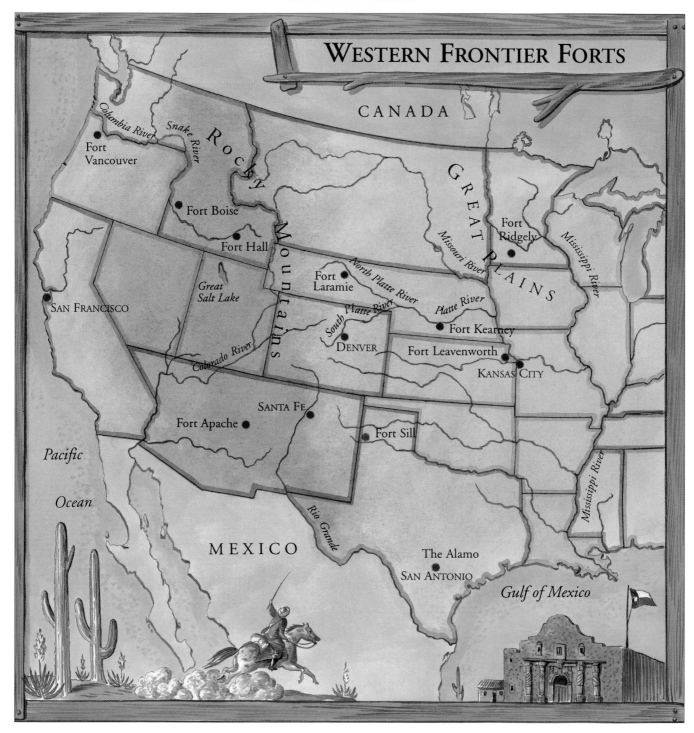

WESTERN FRONTIER FORTS

On the Western frontier, cavalry forts were built along trails to protect settlers as they made their way across the continent.

harbor. Armistead hired Mary Pickersgill who, with the help of her thirteen-year-old daughter Caroline, made the flag in August 1813. Thirty by forty-two feet, the large flag weighed fifty pounds.

After attacking Washington, D.C., and burning the White House and capitol, the British moved on Baltimore. They were halted by Baltimore militia at the Battle of North Point, but on September 13 British warships sailed up Chesapeake Bay and began to shell Fort McHenry. The heavy bombardment continued all day. Meanwhile, Francis Scott Key, a thirty-five-year-old Washington lawyer, had gone to Baltimore to negotiate for the release of an American prisoner. He succeeded, but during the bombardment he was detained on a truce ship anchored eight miles away. At 7:00 A.M. the next day, September 14, 1814, Key glimpsed the American flag still flying proudly over Fort McHenry. He was so inspired that he wrote a poem whose words became the lyrics of our national anthem, "The Star-Spangled Banner."

In the early years of the republic, forts helped the United States to deter the military forces of Britain, France, and Spain—the three great world powers at that time. American forts withstood sieges by pirates in the coastal waters and attacks from Indians in the heart of the wilderness. Forts also played a role in western expansion into Texas and the Southwest. Many people rallied around the defeat at the Alamo to aid Texans in their war of independence against Mexico. This conflict was followed by the Mexican War of 1846–1848, which resulted in the United States taking possession of New Mexico, Arizona, and California.

Forts also figured prominently in the Civil War from the very beginning. After Abraham Lincoln was elected president in 1860, the Southern states, one after the other, seceded from the Union over the issue of slavery and states' rights. Hostilities began in early 1861 at Fort Sumter in South Carolina, which in December 1860 had become the first state to break away. This federal fort, with a small garrison of sixty-eight men under the command of Major Robert Anderson, was on an

The first battle of the Civil War was the Confederate bombardment of Fort Sumter on an island in the harbor of Charleston, South Carolina.

island in the Charleston harbor. In this strategic position, the sturdy, five-sided fort controlled a wide area of land and sea. But Charleston suppliers stopped sending food to the fort.

Although surrounded by six thousand Confederate troops, Major Anderson refused to abandon the fort. At 4:30 A.M. on April 12, 1861, the Confederates began to bombard the stronghold. The siege continued for thirty-four hours, with over three thousand shells exploded around Fort Sumter. Almost miraculously, only one horse was killed, but the rebels also set fire to the fort. Anderson's gunners shot back, but without food or reinforcements they could not hold the fort. Major Anderson requested a truce and reluctantly surrendered. Tragically, one man was killed when Fort Sumter's cannons fired a last salute to the American flag, the only casualty on either side. The garrison were permitted to withdraw from the burning fortress, taking the tattered flag with them.

Confederate forces held Fort Sumter, which was attacked several times by Union ships, nearly until the end of the Civil War. On April 14, 1865, the anniversary of his departure, Major Anderson returned to Fort Sumter and raised the same American flag that he had lowered four years earlier. The same night President Abraham Lincoln went to a play at Ford's Theater in Washington, D.C., and was shot by John Wilkes Booth. If the attack on Fort Sumter started the Civil War, it also fore-shadowed the end of the military value of the fort in North America.

Fort Laramie in Wyoming became a lively gathering place for Indians and traders, as well as soldiers and settlers.

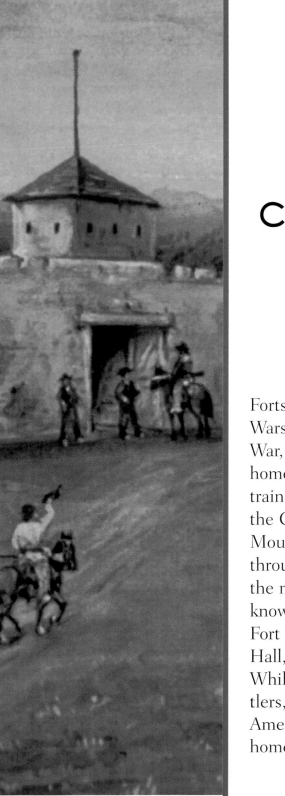

5

CAVALRY FORTS

Forts were still needed in the Indian Wars that lay ahead. After the Civil War, soldiers were sent west to protect homesteaders. By the 1840s, wagon trains had been moving steadily across the Great Plains and through the Rocky Mountains. Cavalry forts were built throughout the West, especially along the major overland trails. The best-known forts of the Oregon Trail were Fort Phil Kearney, Fort Laramie, Fort Hall, Fort Boise, and Fort Vancouver. While these forts offered safety for settlers, they were a threat to Native Americans fighting to defend their homelands and hunting grounds.

After the Civil War, only about 25,000 men remained in the
United States Army. They had to patrol a vast territory from the
Mississippi River to the Pacific Ocean and from Texas to the Canadian
border. In the Far West, from Montana to Arizona, cavalry forts served as
bases for the blue-coated cavalry who rode their sturdy horses over the

wind-swept prairies, deserts, and mountain passes. Less permanent than coastal fortifications, these cavalry forts either led or trailed right behind the waves of pioneers streaming over the continent. The lonely outposts provided military escorts for wagon trains jolting along the dust-choked trails to Oregon and California.

The log walls of cavalry forts offered some protection for settlers on the open plains and deserts of the American West.

Typical of western cavalry forts, Fort Hall in Idaho included living quarters and storerooms within its walls.

Most cavalry forts included one or more two-story blockhouses, usually made of thick logs, where soldiers fought off attackers.

Soldiers at these forts had many duties, primarily defending the trails and the surrounding territory from bands of Indians. Supplied by wagon trains, riverboats, and eventually railroad lines, forts served other purposes as well. Within the forts were often the only doctor and hospital for hundreds of miles. Settlers sought shelter within the palisades or paused to water livestock as their wagon trains rumbled along the

Oregon, Santa Fe, Bozeman, and other trails west. Cavalry forts also became trading posts and stables and housed craftsmen such as black-smiths and wheelwrights. Some of these western forts served as stops for weary stagecoach travelers and as a place where Pony Express riders could exchange horses. Over time, the forts became government centers for dealing with the Indians and for administering the territory. The fort

Headed to Utah in about 1865, a wagon train of Mormon settlers makes its way past Fort Bridger on the Oregon Trail.

commander was the official representative of the United States government—often the only authority in the region. Curiously, these military forts also brought the first libraries, reading rooms, chapels, and schools to many western regions. Military bands often entertained troops and anyone else within earshot. Gardens provided fresh vegetables and pioneered several experiments in American agriculture.

From Texas to North Dakota and from Arizona northward through the Rocky Mountains, cavalry forts reminded native peoples of the great military strength of the United States. Many were intentionally placed in Native American homelands and in buffalo hunting grounds. Fort Sill was built in the land of the Comanche, Fort Apache in the mountains of the Western Apache, and Fort Hall in the territory of the Shoshone. From these forts, soldiers pursued defiant warriors who were brought back for trial and most likely jailed in the stockade, in what served as frontier justice.

In the deserts of the Southwest, where timber was scarce, some forts were built of adobe, but most were made of logs. About 200 by 266 yards, cavalry forts required nearly three thousand timbers for the walls alone. The offices, living quarters, gunpowder magazine, storeroom, stable, and corner blockhouse required additional logs. These forts had at least one blockhouse, which was left open at the top as a command post. The cannon pointed toward the gate as a warning to hostile warriors.

A large fort included the commander's headquarters, officers' quarters, and barracks where the troops slept in bunks. In the mess, soldiers ate stew prepared with dried or salted beef, along with beans and bread. The cooks might occasionally serve wild game, such as buffalo, deer, rabbit, and perhaps fish, as well as vegetables grown in the small garden plots. Soldiers could purchase tobacco and whiskey at the fort store managed by the quartermaster. When not out on patrol, the soldiers drilled on the parade ground beneath the American flag streaming in the breeze.

Native Americans seldom attacked a fort with its thick walls and deadly cannon. Instead, in the Plains style of warfare, they formed small war parties that raided wagon trains or ambushed cavalry patrols. Fort Phil Kearney on the Oregon Trail in Wyoming offers an example of how Native Americans dealt with a cavalry fort in their midst. The fort was well situated near water and grass for grazing livestock. Two nearby hills served as excellent lookout posts. There was plenty of timber near the site planned for the fort. But soldiers had to venture some distance to fell trees and on several occasions, they were attacked.

When the fort was completed on October 31, 1866, it seemed to be very strong. However, the great Sioux chief Red Cloud prevented supplies from getting to the fort through the long winter. The garrison struggled just to stay alive. Without a fort to protect settlers through the following summer, the Oregon Trail had to be closed. On August 2, 1866, the soldiers finally left the fort to help settlers—and Red Cloud promptly led a band of Sioux warriors inside. They burned Fort Phil Kearney to the ground. Its ashes blew away in the high winds of Wyoming. However, this was the only victory of the Plains Indians over a fort of the United States Army.

There were many—perhaps too many—western forts when the Indian Wars finally came to an end in the 1870s. Several, such as Fort Sill in Oklahoma, became military training bases. Others stand as reminders of a time not long ago when buffalo ranged from Ohio to the Rocky Mountains, from Texas to the prairies of Canada. Strangely, once a frontier fort had served its purpose of bringing peace to its territory, it was no longer needed. Once the American frontier, begun on the shores of the Atlantic, ended at the edge of the Pacific Ocean, the nation had become settled, and many forts were abandoned. Over time, the weathered walls and buildings decayed and tumbled down. Yet others, especially those of historic note, have been restored. Today, the National Park Service and state governments care for the remaining forts and historic sites as reminders of the spirit that helped to settle the United States.

GLOSSARY

adobe bricks made of clay and straw dried in the sun

ammunition bullets and gunpowder for firing pistols and rifles

barracks a building where soldiers in a garrison sleep

bastion a projecting part of a fort that helps strengthen the wall

blockhouse a two-story building of heavy timbers that forms part of a fort

cavalry fort a Western fort where cavalry, or soldiers who rode horses, were stationed

dovecote a small, raised house or box, often with compartments, used for raising pigeons

embrasure a window flaring outward in a fort wall through which a cannon is fired

garrison a military post; also the men stationed there

keelboat a shallow riverboat with a keel that is paddled or poled and used for carrying freight

loophole a narrow opening in a fort wall through which guns are fired

magazine a room where gunpowder and other explosives are kept

militia an armed force called into military service during a national emergency

moat a deep, wide trench, often filled with water, around a fort or castle

palisade a vertical log having a pointed end and set close to other palisades to form a wall; a wall built of palisades

parapet a low wall on a platform or a balcony to protect soldiers

revet to make an embankment stronger by covering it with logs or stones

stockade a defensive barrier or wall of posts driven upright into the ground; also a military jail

FURTHER INFORMATION

BOOKS FOR YOUNG READERS

Young readers who would like to learn more about forts may enjoy these fine books:

Day, Malcolm. *Keep Out! The Story of Castles and Forts Through the Ages*. Hemel Hempstead: Macdonald Young Books, 1995.

Giblin, James Cross. *Walls: Defenses Throughout History*. Boston: Little Brown, 1984.

Kalman, Bobbie. *Fort Life*. New York: Crabtree Publishing, 1994.

Owens, Ann-Maureen. *Forts of Canada*. Toronto: Kids Can Press, 1996.

Richardson, Adele. *Frontier Forts*. Mankato, MN: Creative Education, 1999.

Steedman, Scott. *A Frontier Fort on the Oregon Trail*. New York: Peter Bedrick Books, 1993.

Stone, Lynn M. *Forts*. Vero Beach, FL: Rourke Publications, 1993.

Williams, Brian. *Forts & Castles*. New York: Viking, 1994.

WEBSITES

Alphabetical Listing of U.S. Forts
http://members.tripod.com/~dydx/forts/a-z.html

British Forts in North America of the French & Indian War 1754-1763 Period & Earlier
http://fiwar.virtualave.net/forts/british.html

The Center for Fort Preservation and Tourism
http://www.geocities.com/Pentagon/Quarters/1028/forts.html

Fort Phil Kearny / Bozeman Trail Association
http://main.wavecom.net/philkearny/

French Forts in North America of the French & Indian War Period 1754-1763
http://fiwar.virtualave.net/forts/french.html

Historic Western Frontier Forts
http://www.coax.net/people/lwf/wf_forts.htm

Links to Old West Forts and Towns
http://www.over-land.com/westfort.html

Mackinac State Historic Parks
http://www.mackinac.com/historicparks/FortMackinac/index.html

N.A. Forts Related Links
http://www.geocities.com/naforts/links.htm

North American Fortifications
http://www.geocities.com/naforts/forts.htm

Old Fort William
http://www.oldfortwilliam.on.ca/homepage.html

Ultimate U.S. Forts Links Page
http://dydx.tripod.com/forts/

BIBLIOGRAPHY

The following books were consulted while researching and writing *The Forts*:

Brice, Martin. *Forts and Fortresses: From the Hillforts of Prehistory to Modern Times, the Definitive Visual Account of the Science of Fortification.* New York: Facts on File, 1990.

Forts & Battlefields. Pleasantville, NY: Reader's Digest, 1997.

Haas, Irvin. *Citadels, Ramparts & Stockades: America's Historic Forts.* New York: Everest House, 1979.

Hinds, James R. *Bulwark and Bastion: a Look at Musket Era Fortifications with a Glance at Period Siegecraft.* Revised ed. Union City, TN: Pioneer Press, 1996.

Pangallo, Michelle M. *North American Forts and Fortifications.* Cambridge; New York: Cambridge University Press, 1986.

Roberts, Robert B. *Encyclopedia of Historic Forts: The Military, Pioneer, and Trading Posts of the United States.* New York: Macmillan, 1988.

Starbuck, David R. *The Great Warpath: British Military Sites from Albany to Crown Point.* Hanover, NH: University Press of New England, 1999.

Swartley, Ron. *Old Forts of the Apache Wars: a Travel Guide.* Las Cruces, NM: Frontier Image Press, 1999.

INDEX

*Page numbers in **boldface** are illustrations*

Raymond Bial has published over fifty critically acclaimed books of non-fiction and fiction for children and adults. His photo essays for children include *Corn Belt Harvest, County Fair, Amish Home, Cajun Home, Frontier Home, Shaker Home, The Underground Railroad, Portrait of a Farm Family, With Needle and Thread: A Book About Quilts, Mist Over the Mountains: Appalachia and Its People, The Strength of These Arms: Life in the Slave Quarters, Where Lincoln Walked, One-Room School, A Handful of Dirt,* and *Ghost Towns of the American West.*

He has written Lifeways, a series published by Marshall Cavendish about Native Americans, traveling to tribal cultural centers, to photograph people, places, and objects that reflect the rich history and social life of Indian peoples.

Building America is the author's second series with Marshall Cavendish. As with his other work, Bial's love of social and cultural history and his deep feeling for his subjects is evident in both the text and the illustrations.

A full-time librarian at a small college in Champaign, Illinois, he lives with his wife and three children in nearby Urbana.